*S*hipwrecks
around Land's End

Richard and Bridget Larn

Tor Mark Press • Redruth

THE TOR MARK SERIES

Maritime interest

Charlestown
Cornish fishing industry
Cornish smuggling industry
Cornwall's early lifeboats
Harry Carter – Cornish smuggler
Lost ports of Cornwall
Shipwrecks around Land's End

Shipwrecks around the Lizard
Shipwrecks around Mount's Bay
Shipwrecks – Falmouth to Looe
Strange tales of the Cornish coast
Tales of the Cornish fishermen
Tales of the Cornish smugglers
Tales of the Cornish wreckers

Other titles

China clay
Classic Cornish anecdotes
Classic Cornish ghost stories
Classic Devon ghost stories
Classic West Country ghost stories
Cornish fairies
Cornish folklore
Cornish legends
Cornish mining – at surface
Cornish mining – underground
Cornish mining industry
Cornish recipes
Cornish saints
Cornwall in camera
Cornwall's engine houses
Cornwall's railways
Customs and superstitions from
  Cornish folklore
Demons, ghosts and spectres in
  Cornish folklore

Devonshire customs and
  superstitions
Devonshire jokes and stories
Devonshire legends
Do you know Cornwall?
Down 'long weth we
Exploring Cornwall with your car
Houses, castles and gardens
  in Cornwall
Introducing Cornwall
King Arthur – man or myth?
Old Cornwall – in pictures
The pasty book
The pixy book
The story of Cornwall
The story of the Cornish language
The story of St Ives
The story of Truro Cathedral
Tales of the Cornish miners
Twelve walks on the Lizard

Published by Tor Mark Press
United Downs Industrial Estate, St Day, Redruth, Cornwall TR16 5HY
First published 1989. Reprinted 1992 and 1997

© 1989 Tor Mark Press
ISBN 0-85025-307-1

Acknowledgement is gratefully given to the many early photographers of
shipwrecks in Cornwall whose collections have made this book possible,
particularly four generations of the Gibson family of Penzance and the Isles of
Scilly; Richard Bros. also of Penzance; and the Hawkes of Helston.

The map on page 3 was drawn by Delta Graphics.

Printed in Great Britain by Burstwick Print and Publicity Services, Hull

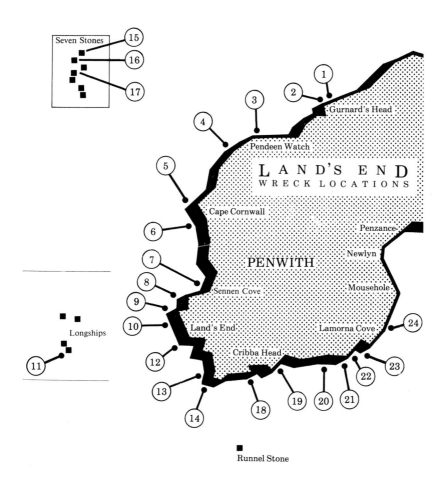

Seven Stones

15
16
17

1
2 Gurnard's Head
3
4 Pendeen Watch
5
Cape Cornwall

L AND'S E N D
W R E C K   L O C A T I O N S

Penzance

Newlyn

PENWITH

Mousehole

6
7
8 Sennen Cove
9
Longships
10 Land's End
11
12
Cribba Head
13
14
18
19 20 21
22
23
24 Lamorna Cove

Runnel Stone

1 Traute Sarnow
2 Alexander Yeats
3 Paknam
4 William Cory, Liberty
  and Alacrity
5 Malta
6 L-1 and Ravenshoe
7 unnamed barge
8 Jean Gougy, Nefeli and
  Lavarenne

9 Mellanear
10 Lambaness
11 Bluejacket
12 Balbec
13 Khyber
14 J Duncan
15 Longships
16 Torrey Canyon
17 Ra-Rau

18 Benwick aand Vert
   Prairial
19 St Guenole
20 South America,
   Abertay and Saintonge
21 Juan Ferrer
22 Avebury
23 Lady of the Isles
24 Ansgir

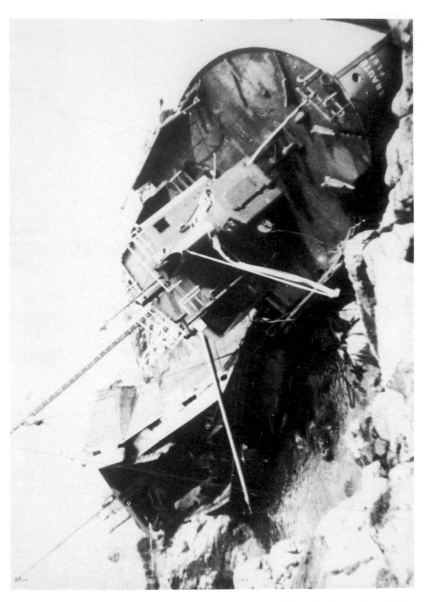

The 229 ton coaster *Traute Sarnow*, carrying anthracite from Cardiff to Ostend, was wrecked in fog below Gurnard's Head on 28 July 1954. Her young German crew and Captain Gustav Sarnow were rescued from the cliff top by breeches buoy.

The largest sailing ship ever lost between Land's End and St Ives was the *Alexander Yeats*, a 1589 ton barque. Her cargo of timber shifted so that she listed heavily to port, and she was blown ashore under Gurnard's Head on 25 September 1896.

Only three days out from the Clyde on her maiden voyage bound for Le Havre, the 200 ton river steamship *Paknam* was wrecked at Greeb Point on 13 May 1895.

The *William Cory*, 1592 tons, was carrying pit props from Finland to Newport when she went ashore under the Levant mine workings at Pendeen on 18 September 1910. Conditions were described as 'a fine, clear summer's morning without a breath of wind'.

The Liberian registered *Liberty* was a 5250 ton tramp steamer, built in 1918 as the *War Camel* and later renamed *Cairndhu* and then *Styrmion*. She suffered engine failure on 17 January 1952 in a gale and was driven shore under Pendeen Watch. The crew of thirty-five were saved by breeches buoy.

The coaster *Alacrity*, bound from Swansea to Brussels with a cargo of anthracite dust, was stranded in Portheras Cove in dense fog on 13 September 1963. Salvage operations failed to refloat her and within weeks she was in three pieces. By December she had virtually disappeared.

Built in an era when steamships still resembled sailing ships, with bowsprit and figurehead, the 2244 ton Cunard liner *Malta* was bound from Liverpool to Genoa when she went ashore under Kenidjack castle, half a mile east of Cape Cornwall, on 15 October 1889.

HM Submarine L-1 was a veteran of World War I. She broke adrift from her tug while being towed from Chatham dockyard to the breaker's yard at Newport, and went ashore at Perranwell Cove, Cape Cornwall, arousing even more curiosity than wrecks usually do.

Engine failure caused the 3592 ton collier *Ravenshoe* to drift ashore below Carn Gloose on New Year's Day 1920. All 27 crew were rescued by the Sennen Cove rocket brigade from the clifftop.

This un-named barge broke adrift from her tow in April 1973; she was refloated and saved.

The Cypriot motor vessel *Nefeli* was stranded in Dollar Cove, Gamper Bay, close to the Irish Lady Rock on 5 November 1972. Winter gales swiftly destroyed her, and by the following June only her bow remained intact.

A remarkable incident following the wreck on 3 November 1962 of the Dieppe trawler *Jean Gougy*, in which 11 men died, has given it a place in Cornish history. Six men were spotted on the bridge; it was impossible to rescue them immediately and they were presumed drowned when the vessel was submerged by the tide for six hours, but five of them survived in an air pocket and were brought to safety by breeches buoy and a helicopter.

The Penzance registered *Mellanear*, 438 tons, ran into dense fog off Land's End on 28 September 1928 and struck the Peal Rocks. The sea broke her back and she became a total loss.

Incredible though it may seem, the Cardiff tramp steamer *Bluejacket* ended up high and dry on the Longships Reef less than twenty yards from the lighthouse door!

This was on 9 November 1898. She was in ballast after delivering a cargo of railway sleepers from Danzig to Plymouth.

Balbec

Above: an early Cunard vessel, the *Balbec*, struck a submerged object near the Longships and had to be run ashore in Nanjizel Bay on 28 March 1884; her twenty-nine crew and five passengers were landed safely.

Left: a victim of Gamper Bay under the high cliffs of Land's End, the *Lavarenne* went aground on 20 September 1973 and sat on top of the rusting remains of the *Jean Gougy* and *Nefeli* – but not for long: the lower picture shows the same spot just one week later.

Above: perhaps the worst shipwreck of all near Land's End, the full-rigged ship *Khyber* was seen to be in difficulties in the rising gale at nightfall on 14 March 1905. At first light she was almost ashore in Portloe, then in just fifteen minutes she went to pieces. Only three were rescued from a crew of twenty-six.

Left: under charter to the Admiralty to carry coal from her home port of Cardiff to Devonport Dockyard, the 1939 ton *J Duncan* ran ashore below Carn Guthenbras during the early hours of 14 August 1913. Naval tugs, a destroyer and local lifeboats all failed to pull her clear of the rocks.

Benwick.

The 2773 ton *Benwick* of Liverpool, bound from Antwerp to Swansea in ballast, struck the offshore Runnelstone Rock in thick fog on 11 February 1903. Twenty-four of the crew took to the boats and the Sennen lifeboat saved five left on board. She drifted ashore near Porthcurno.

Another Land's End tragedy, the French trawler *Vert Prairial* was
found like this under Pedn-Men-an-Mere Point near Porthcurno at
dawn on 14 March 1956. There was no sign of survivors from her 17
crew, and what exactly happened remains a mystery.

Above: the first of the world's supertanker disasters, the 118 285 ton deadweight *Torrey Canyon* was wrecked on the Seven Stones reef on 18 March 1967, while carrying 120 000 tons of crude oil. Severe pollution affected the whole of south-west Cornwall, with oil eighteen inches deep on some beaches. When she broke into three pieces, the vessel was bombed by order of the government to try to set the oil on fire.

Left: the Romanian fish factory ship *Ra-Rau* was stranded on the Seven Stones reef in September 1976 and broke her back. All 84 crew were rescued.

Above: it was the strong smell of fuel oil, then the sighting of a man in the shallows of Penberth Cove, that alerted the coastguards to the wreck of the tar tanker *St Guenole* of Rouen, which was later found upside down under Gribba Point on 1 November 1948. There was just one survivor from a crew of twelve.

Left: the Clyde Shipping Company steamer *Longships*, carrying a general cargo from Belfast to Plymouth, was stranded on the Seven Stones reef on 22 December 1939 and broke her back.

This extraordinary incident occurred in 1912. On 13 March the 4197 ton *South America* went ashore in fog; her crew rowed themselves ashore and her steel hull was still intact when, on 14 October, the 599 ton *Abertay* crashed into the wreck and came to rest so neatly positioned that it could have been deliberate!

News that the French steamer *Saintonge* had been wrecked in St Loy Bay came from a labourer woken in his clifftop cottage by the crash as she hit the rocks, on 21 March 1895. Her crew and cargo of pit-props were saved, but the vessel was a wreck.

A new lighthouse was built on Tater Du headland as a direct result of the wreck of the Spanish coaster *Juan Ferrer*, at the foot of Boscawen Cliff on 23 October 1963, when 11 of her 15 crew lost their lives.

Carrying a full cargo of iron ore and esparto grass from Lisbon to Cardiff, the Sunderland owned steamship *Avebury* miscalculated her position when trying to round Land's End in fog, and drove ashore under Rosemodress Cliff, half a mile south of Lamorna Cove, on 28 October 1884.

The *Lady of the Isles* was the regular packet steamer between Penzance and Scilly but she also undertook occasional sightseeing trips. She struck a rock ledge close to Carn-du and had to be run ashore at Lamorna Cove on 1 September 1904, to save her sinking. Three large holes were repaired and she returned to service, being finally lost off Falmouth in 1940.

The 6483 ton *Ansgir* was of German origin, having been surrendered to the British after World War 1, and was on her way to Barry to load coal for the Far East, where she was to be handed over to the Japanese, when she went ashore on Penzer Point on 1 December 1920 and was wrecked.